Hal Leonard
Bass Method
Supplement to Any Bass Method

Easy Pop Bass Lines

INTRODUCTION

Welcome to *Easy Pop Bass Lines*, a collection of 20 pop and rock favorites arranged for easy bass. If you're a beginning bassist, you've come to the right place; these well-known songs will have you playing, reading, and enjoying music in no time!

This book can be used on its own or as a supplement to the *Hal Leonard Bass Method* or any other beginning bass method. The songs are arranged in order of difficulty, beginning with basic concepts and progressing to more challenging rhythms and fingerings. Each bass line is presented in an easy-to-read format—including lyrics to help you follow along and chords for optional accompaniment (by your teacher, if you have one).

ISBN 978-0-634-07021-1

7777 W. BLUEMOUND RD. P.O. BOX 13819 MILWAUKEE, WI 53213

Visit Hal Leonard Online at
www.halleonard.com

SONG STRUCTURE

The songs in this book have different sections, which may or may not include the following:

Intro
This is usually a short instrumental section that "introduces" the song at the beginning.

Verse
This is one of the main sections of a song and conveys most of the storyline. A song usually has several verses, all with the same music but each with different lyrics.

Chorus
This is often the most memorable section of a song. Unlike the verse, the chorus usually has the same lyrics every time it repeats.

Bridge
This section is a break from the rest of the song, often having a very different chord progression and feel.

Solo
This is an instrumental section, often played over the verse or chorus structure.

Outro
Similar to an intro, this section brings the song to an end.

ENDINGS & REPEATS

Many of the songs have some new symbols that you must understand before playing. Each of these represents a different type of ending.

1st and 2nd Endings
These are indicated by brackets and numbers. The first time through a song section, play the first ending and then repeat. The second time through, skip the first ending, and play through the second ending.

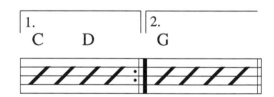

D.S.
This means "Dal Segno" or "from the sign." When you see this abbreviation above the staff, find the sign (𝄋) earlier in the song and resume playing from that point.

al Coda
This means "to the Coda," a concluding section in the song. If you see the words "D.S. al Coda," return to the sign (𝄋) earlier in the song and play until you see the words "To Coda," then skip to the Coda at the end of the song, indicated by the symbol: ⊕.

al Fine
This means "to the end." If you see the words "D.S. al Fine," return to the sign (𝄋) earlier in the song and play until you see the word "Fine."

D.C.
This means "Da Capo" or "from the head." When you see this abbreviation above the staff, return to the beginning (or "head") of the song and resume playing.

CONTENTS

IMAGINE

Words and Music by
JOHN LENNON

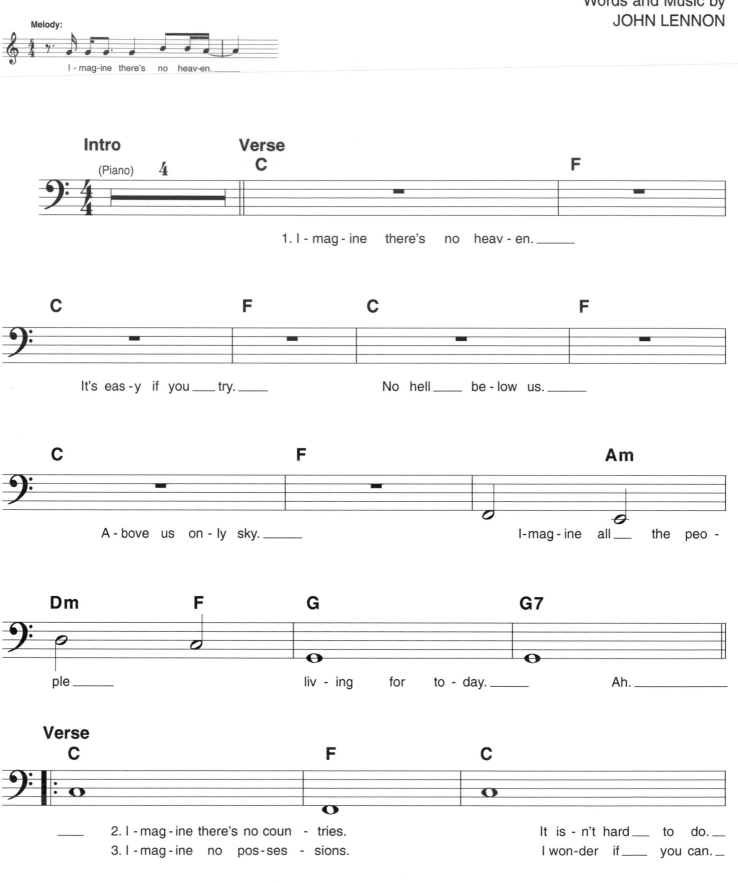

I - mag-ine there's no heav-en.

Intro
(Piano)

Verse
C   F

1. I - mag - ine there's no heav - en. _____

C   F   C   F

It's eas-y if you ____ try. ____   No hell ____ be-low us. ____

C   F   Am

A - bove us on - ly sky. _____   I-mag-ine all ___ the peo -

Dm   F   G   G7

ple _____   liv - ing for to - day. _____   Ah. _____

Verse
C   F   C

____ 2. I - mag - ine there's no coun - tries.   It is - n't hard ___ to do. ___
        3. I - mag - ine no pos-ses - sions.   I won-der if ____ you can. ___

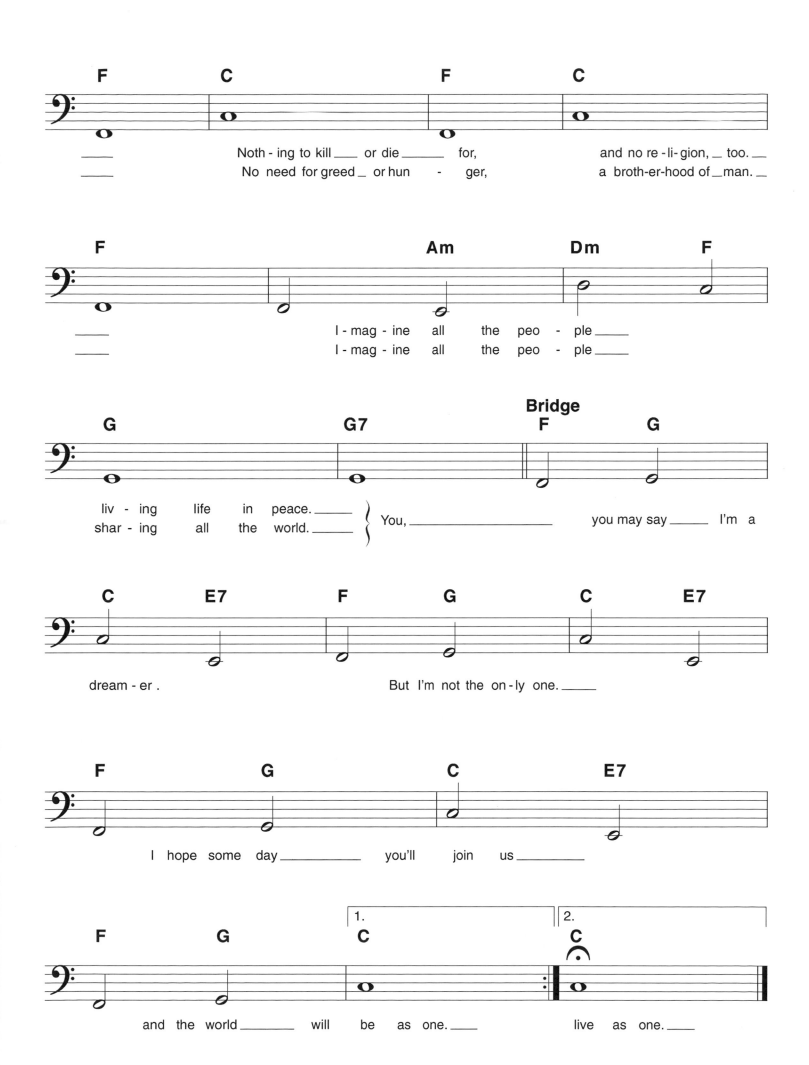

A WHITER SHADE OF PALE

Words and Music by
KEITH REID and GARY BROOKER

1. We   skipped the light __ fan - dan - go, _____
2. She   said, "I'm home __ on   shore leave," _____
3. She   said, "There is __ no   rea - son, _____

F   **F/E**   **Dm7**

turned cart - wheels   'cross the floor; _____
through in truth we _____ were at sea; _____
and the truth is _____ plain to see," _____

G   **G/F**   **Em**   **G7**

I was feel-ing kind of sea - sick,
so I took her by the look-ing glass
but I wan-dered through my play-ing cards

C   **C/B**   **Am**   **Em**

the crowd called out _____ for more.
and forced her to _____ a - gree.
and would not let _____ her be

F   **Dm/E**   **Dm7**

The room was hum - ming hard - er
Say - ing, "You must be the mer - maid
one of six - teen ves - tal vir - gins

G   **G/F**   **Em**   **G7**

as the ceil - ing flew a - way. _____
who took Nep - tune for a ride," _____
who were leav - ing for the coast. _____

C   **C/B**   **Am**   **Em**

When we called out for an - oth - er drink _____
but she smiled at me so sad - ly _____
And al - though my eyes were o - pen _____

WONDERFUL TONIGHT

Words and Music by
Eric Clapton

It's late in the eve - ning.

Intro

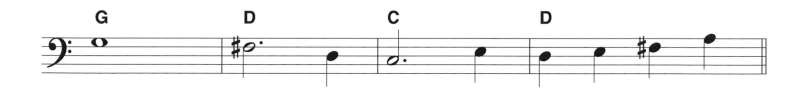

Verse

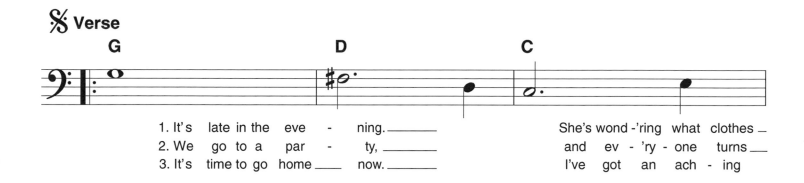

1. It's late in the eve - ning. _____ She's wond -'ring what clothes ___
2. We go to a par - ty, _____ and ev - 'ry - one turns ___
3. It's time to go home ____ now. _____ I've got an ach - ing

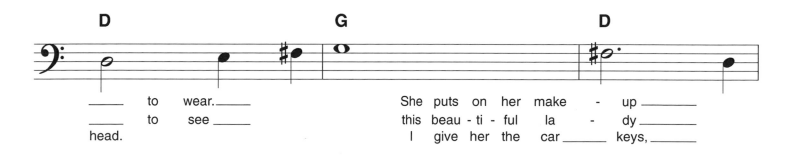

_____ to wear. _____ She puts on her make - up _____
_____ to see ____ this beau - ti - ful la - dy _____
head. I give her the car ____ keys, _____

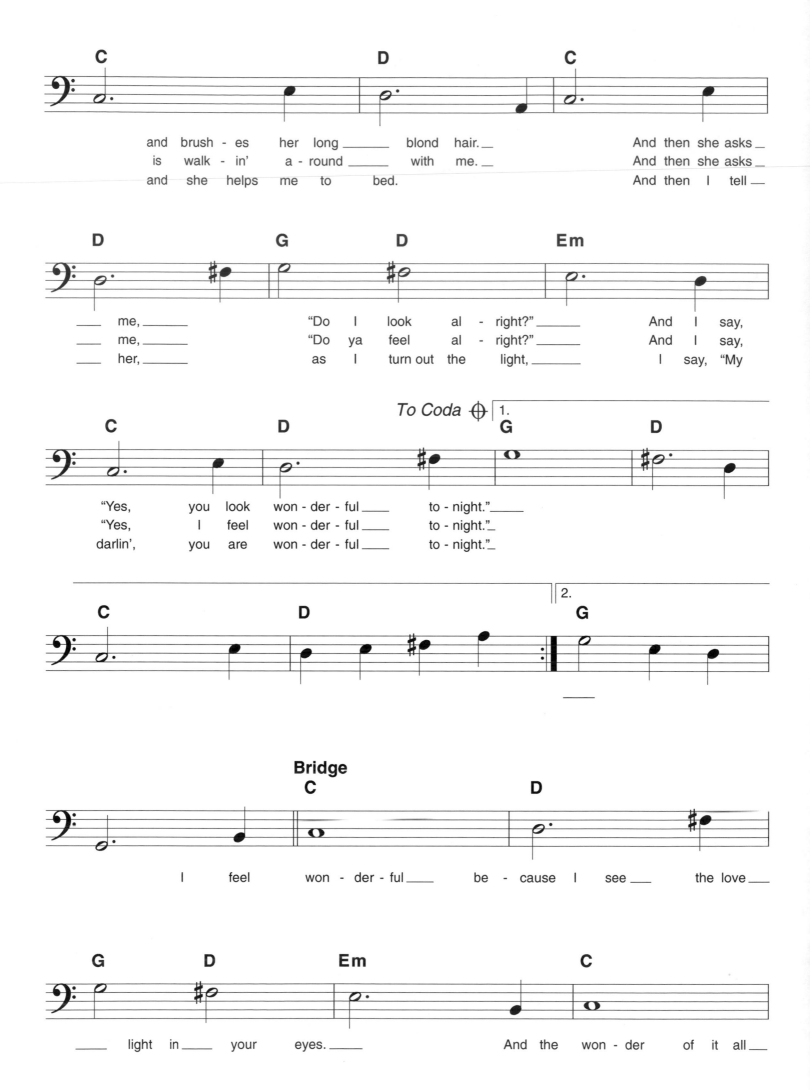

and brush - es her long _____ blond hair. __ And then she asks _
is walk - in' a - round _____ with me. __ And then she asks _
and she helps me to bed. And then I tell —

___ me, _____ "Do I look al - right?" _____ And I say,
___ me, _____ "Do ya feel al - right?" _____ And I say,
___ her, _____ as I turn out the light, _____ I say, "My

To Coda ⊕ | 1.

"Yes, you look won - der - ful ___ to - night." ___
"Yes, I feel won - der - ful ___ to - night." ___
darlin', you are won - der - ful ___ to - night." __

| 2.

Bridge

I feel won - der - ful ___ be - cause I see ___ the love ___

___ light in ___ your eyes. ___ And the won - der of it all ___

is that you just don't re - al - ize how much I love you.

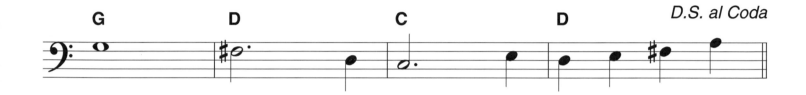

D.S. al Coda

Oh, my dar - lin', you are

won - der - ful to - night.

LADY MADONNA

Words and Music by
JOHN LENNON and PAUL McCARTNEY

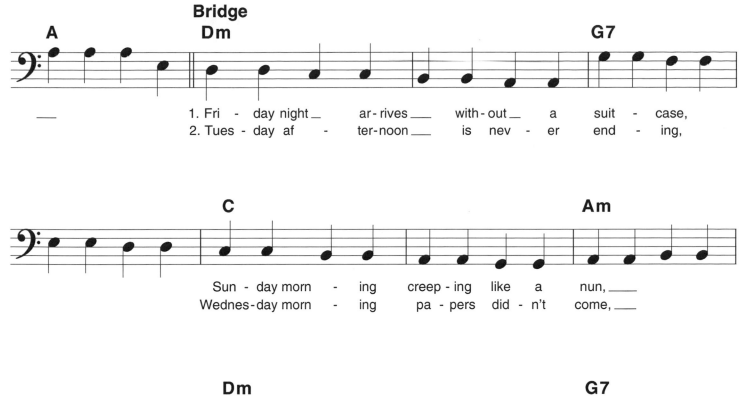

Bridge

A | Dm | | G7

1. Fri - day night __ ar - rives __ with - out __ a suit - case,
2. Tues - day af - ter-noon __ is nev - er end - ing,

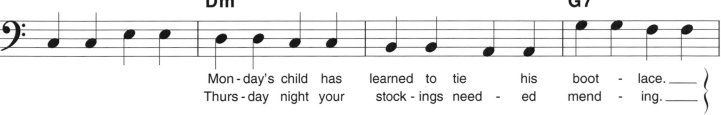

C | | | Am

Sun - day morn - ing creep - ing like a nun, ____
Wednes-day morn - ing pa - pers did - n't come, ____

Dm | | | G7

Mon - day's child has learned to tie his boot - lace. ____
Thurs - day night your stock - ings need - ed mend - ing. ____

D.S. al Coda

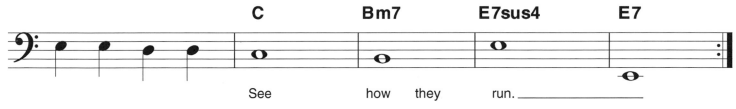

C | Bm7 | E7sus4 | E7

See how they run. _____

⊕ *Coda*

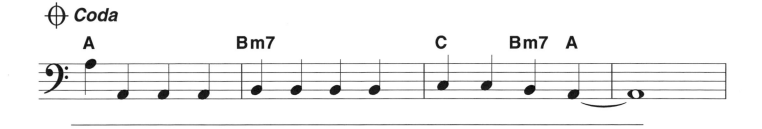

A | Bm7 | C | Bm7 A

Bm7 | C | Bm7 A

13

Peggy Sue

Words and Music by JERRY ALLISON,
NORMAN PETTY and BUDDY HOLLY

pret - ty , pret - ty, pret - ty, pret - ty Peg - gy Sue.____ Oh, oh Peg - gy,

my Peg - gy Sue._____ Oh well, I

To Coda ⊕

love you gal,_ and I need you Peg - gy Sue.____

Guitar Solo

D.S. al Coda

I love you, ____ Peg - gy Sue, ____ with a love so

rare and true, ____ oh ____ Peg - gy, my Peg - gy Sue -

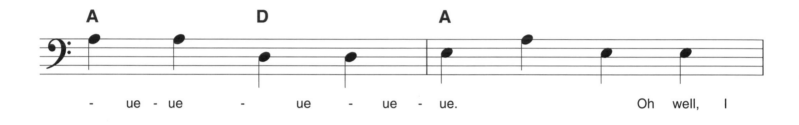

- ue - ue - ue - ue - ue. Oh well, I

love you gal, ____ and I want you Peg - gy Sue. _____

Oh well, I love ____ you gal, ____ and I

want you Peg - gy Sue. ____

WALK OF LIFE

Words and Music by
MARK KNOPFLER

Melody:

Here comes John - ny sing-ing old - ies, gold - ies.

Intro

(Guitar & kybd.)

E A

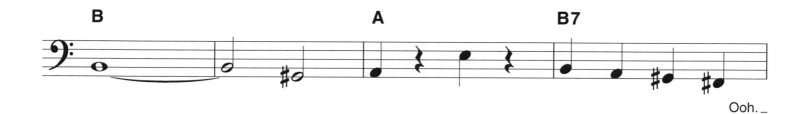

B A B7

Ooh.

E A

Ooh.   Ooh.

B A B7

Verse

E

1. Here comes John - ny sing-ing old - ies, gold - ies.
2. Here comes John - ny gon - na tell you the sto - ry.

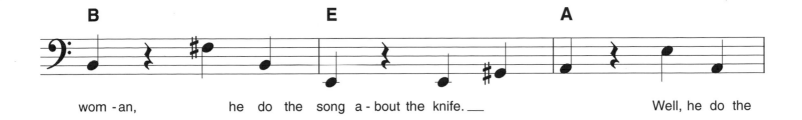

wom -an, he do the song a - bout the knife. __ Well, he do the

walk, do the walk of life. _____ Yeah!_

Interlude

__ He do the walk of life. _____

Ooh. _____

Ooh. _____

Repeat and fade

TENNESSEE WALTZ

Words and Music by
REDD STEWART and PEE WEE KING

TAKIN' CARE OF BUSINESS

Words and Music by
RANDY BACHMAN

SURFIN' U.S.A.

Words and Music by
CHUCK BERRY

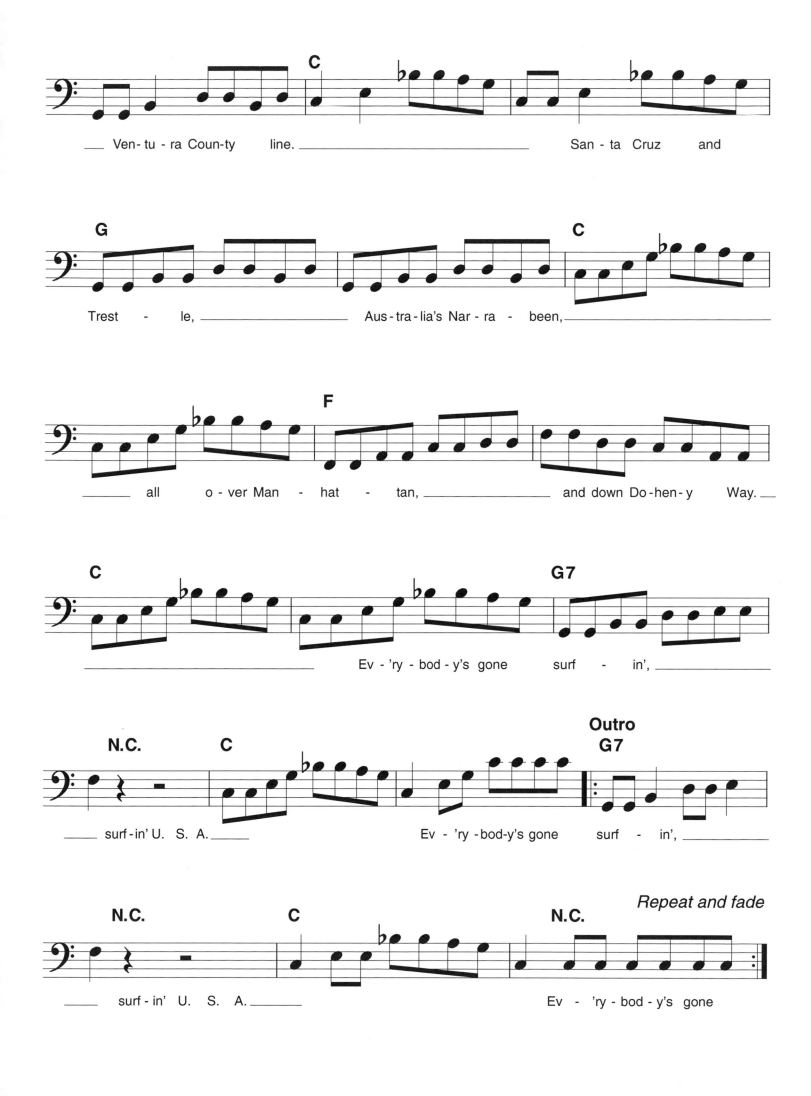

All The Small Things

Words and Music by
TOM De LONGE and MARK HOPPUS

Melody:

All the ___ small things. ___

Intro

1. All the ___

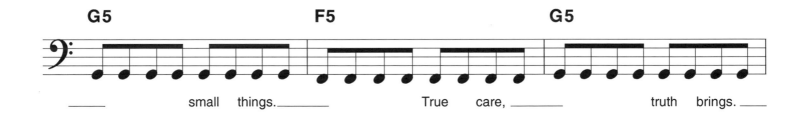

___ small things. ___ True care, ___ truth brings. ___

___ I'll take ___ one lift. ___ Your ride, ___

___ best trip. ___ Al - ways, ___ I know ___

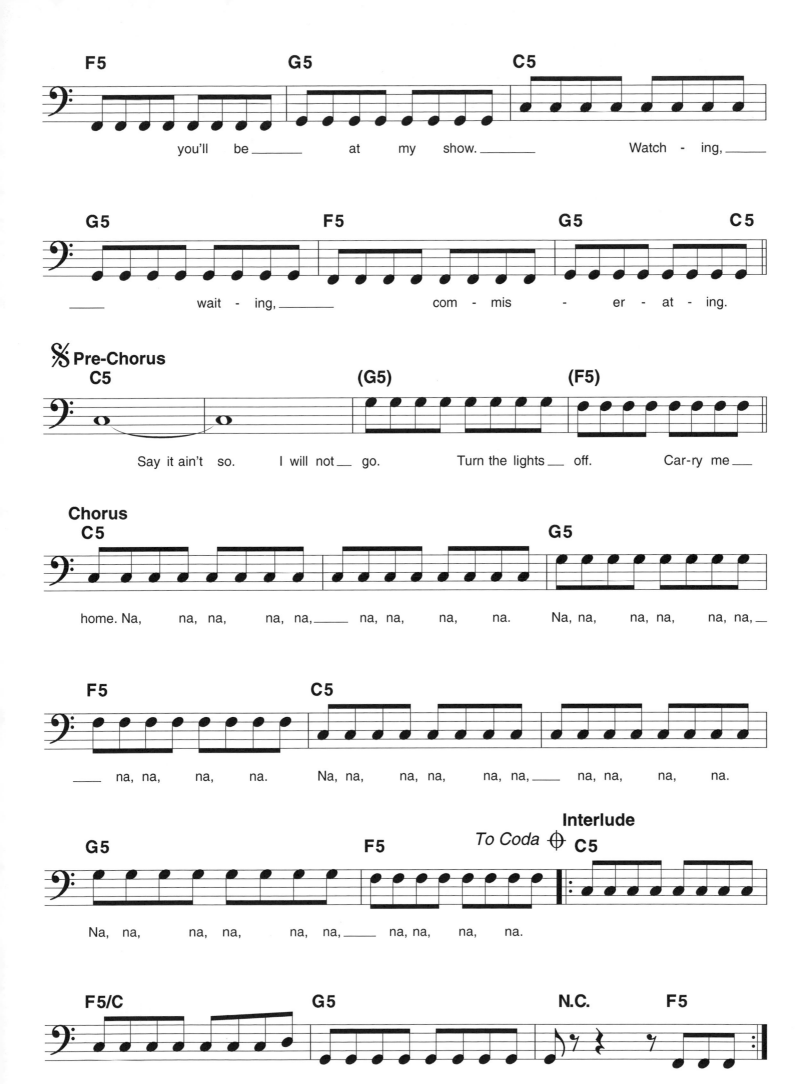

Verse

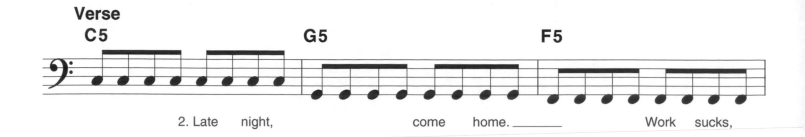

2. Late night, come home. _____ Work sucks,

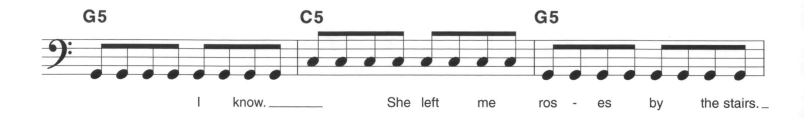

I know. _____ She left me ros - es by the stairs. _

D.S. al Coda

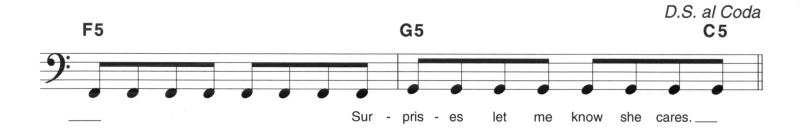

_____ Sur - pris - es let me know she cares. ___

Coda

Play 3 times

Outro

Say it ain't so. I will not ___

28

WILD THING

Words and Music by
CHIP TAYLOR

Melody:

Wild thing, you make my...

Intro

N.C.   A   D   E

Chorus

A   D

Wild thing,

E   D   A   D   E   D

you make my heart sing.   You make ev-

A   D   E   D   A   D

-'ry-thing groov - y. _____   Wild thing.

𝄋 Verse

Gsus4 A Gsus4   A   Gsus4 A Gsus4

1. Wild thing, ____ I   think I love you,
2. Wild thing, ____ I   think you move me,

A   Gsus4 A Gsus4 A

but I wan - na know ____ for sure.   So come on and

Outro-Chorus

Begin fade

Wild thing, you make my heart sing.

You make ev - 'ry - thing groov - y. ____

Fade out

Wild thing. Come on, ___ come on wild thing.

COME AS YOU ARE

Words and Music by
KURT COBAIN

Come as you are, _____

Intro

(Guitar) N.C. (F♯m) (E) (F♯m) (E)

(F♯m) (E) (F♯m)

Verse

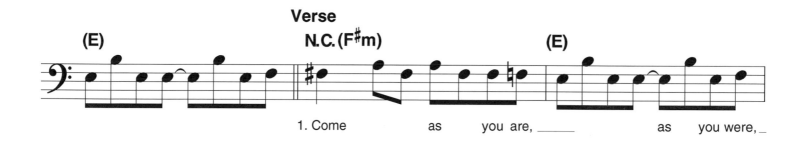

(E) N.C. (F♯m) (E)

1. Come as you are, _____ as you were, _

(F♯m) (E) (F♯m)

___ as I want ___ you ___ to be; _____ as a friend, _

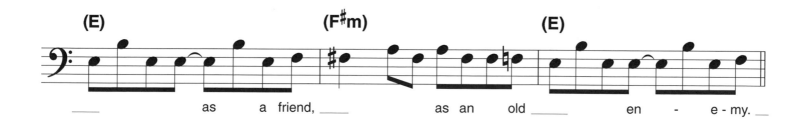

(E) (F♯m) (E)

___ as a friend, _____ as an old _____ en - e - my. _

_____ Take your time, _____ hur - ry up, ___
2. Come doused in mud, _____ soaked in bleach, __

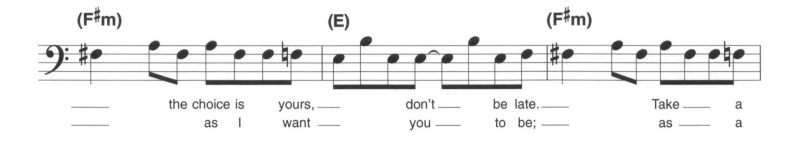

_____ the choice is yours, ___ don't ___ be late.___ Take ___ a
_____ as I want ___ you ___ to be; ___ as ___ a

rest, } as a friend, _____ as an old _____ mem - o - ry, __
trend, }

Chorus

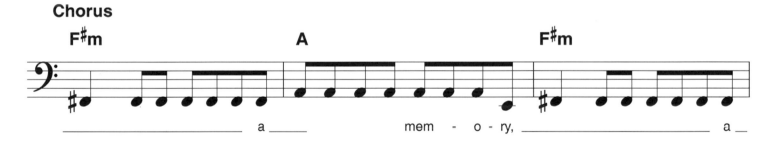

F#m   A   F#m

_____ a _____ mem - o - ry, _____ a __

A   F#m   A

_____ mem - o - ry, _____ a _____ mem - o - ry, __

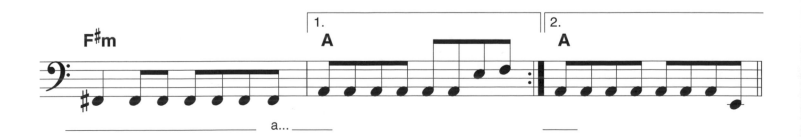

F#m   1. A   2. A

_____ a... _____

Bridge

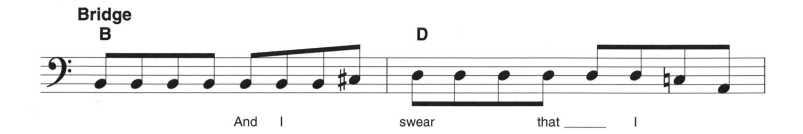

And I   swear   that _____ I

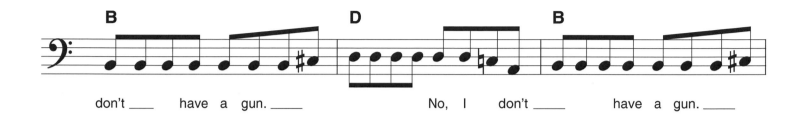

don't ____ have a gun. _____   No, I don't _____   have a gun. _____

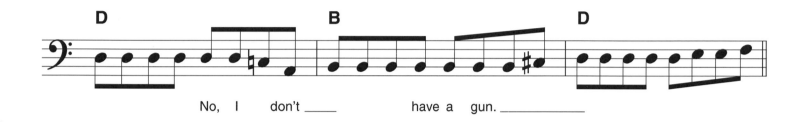

No, I don't _____   have a gun. _____

Guitar Solo

Outro

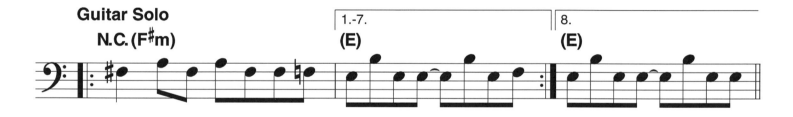

Mem - o - ry, ____

_____ a... _____

GREAT BALLS OF FIRE

Words and Music by
OTIS BLACKWELL and JACK HAMMER

Melody:

You shake my nerves and you rat - tle my brain.

Verse
C

1. You shake my nerves and you rat - tle my brain.

F7   **G7**

Too much love drives a man in - sane. ___   You broke my will,

F7   **C**   **N.C.**

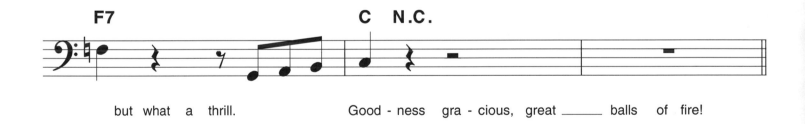

but what a thrill.   Good - ness gra - cious, great ___ balls of fire!

Verse
C

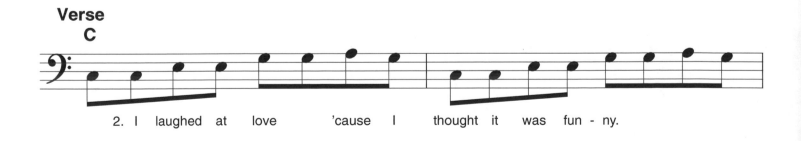

2. I laughed at love 'cause I thought it was fun - ny.

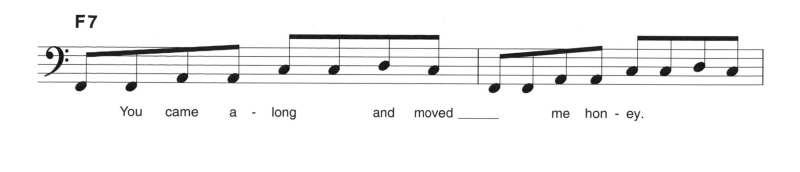

F7

You came a - long and moved _____ me hon - ey.

G7 **F7**

I changed my mind, this love is fine.

C N.C. **Bridge** **F7**

Good - ness gra - cious, great _____ balls of fire! Kiss me ba - by,

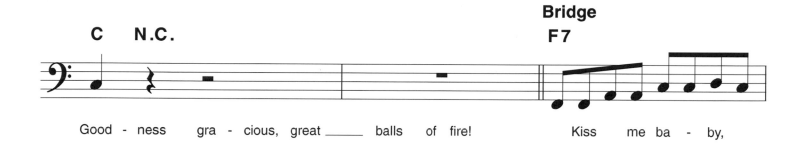

C

hmmm *feels* *good.*

F7 **G7**

Hold me, ba - by! Well, _____ I wan - na love ya like a

lov - er should. ___   You're fine, ___   so kind. ___   I

G7   **Verse**
C

got to tell this world that you're mine, mine, mine, mine.   3. I chew my nails and I

F7

twid - dle   my thumbs.   I'm real ner - vous   but it

G7   **F7**

sure is fun. __   Come on ba - by,   you drive me cra - zy,

C **N.C.**   **C**

good - ness   gra - cious, great _____ balls   of   fire!

MY GIRL

Words and Music by
WILLIAM "SMOKEY" ROBINSON and RONALD WHITE

Melody:

I've got sun - shine

Intro

N.C. (C)

Verse

C5   F

1. I've got sun - shine   on a cloud -

C5   F   C5

- y day.   When it's cold out - side,

F   C5   F5

I've got the month of May.

C5   **F**   **Dm**

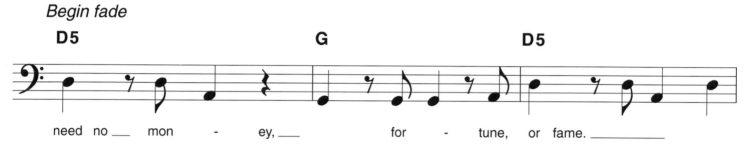

G   **Em**   **A**

Oo, _____ yeah. __   2. I ___ don't

Verse

Begin fade

D5   **G**   **D5**

need no __ mon - ey, __   for - tune, or fame. _____

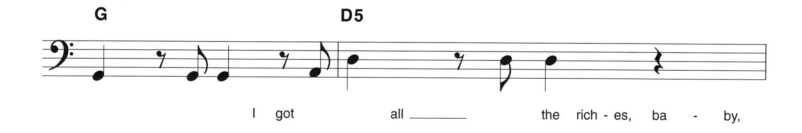

G   **D5**

I got   all _____ the rich - es, ba - by,

Fade out

G   **D5**   **G**

one man _____ can claim. _____   Well, ____

I CAN'T HELP MYSELF
(SUGAR PIE, HONEY BUNCH)

Words and Music by BRIAN HOLLAND,
LAMONT DOZIER and EDWARD HOLLAND

Melody:

Sug - ar pie hon - ey bunch,...

Intro
N.C.(C)

Oo.

Verse
C   G

1. Sug - ar pie hon - ey bunch, you know that I ___ love you. ___

Dm   G/E

I can't help my - self. I love ___ you and

F   G   C6   C

no - bod - y else. ___ In ___ and out my life,

you come and you go ____   leav-ing ____ just ____ your

pic-ture be-hind. _____   And I kissed it a thou-sand times. ____

2. When ____ you snap your fin-ger or wink your ____ eyes, ____ I come a

run-nin' to you. ____   I'm tied ____ to your a-pron string _____

and there's noth-ing ____ that I can ____ do. ____   Oo. ____   3. Sug-

-ar pie hon-ey bunch,   I'm weak-er than a

G   Dm

man   should be. ____   I can't   help   my - self ____

                           G/E   F   G   C6

I'm a fool ____ in ____ love, ____ you see. ____   Wan-na tell __

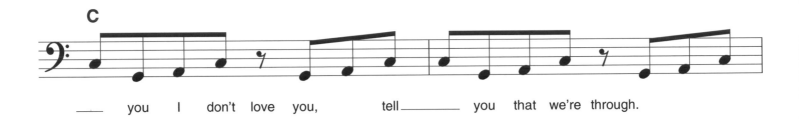

C

____ you   I don't love you,   tell_____ you   that we're through.

G

And   I've   tried, _____   but   ev - 'ry   time ___   I

Begin fade

Dm   G/E

see   your   face_____   I   get all _____   choked

Fade out

F   G   C6

up   in - side. _____   When___

Dancing in the Street

Words and Music by MARVIN GAYE,
IVY HUNTER and WILLIAM STEVENSON

danc - ing __ in the street. __ They're danc-ing in Chi - ca - go, __
danc - ing __ in the street. __ Phil - a - del- phia, P. A., _____

down in New Or - leans, _____ in New York __ Cit -
Bal-ti-more and D. C., now. _____ Can't for - get the Mo - tor Cit -

A

y.
y.

All _____ we need _____ is mu - sic, sweet __ mu -

- sic. There'll __ be mu - sic ev - 'ry - where. __

E7

___ There'll __ be swing - ing, sway - ing and

rec - ords play - ing, danc - ing __ in the street, _____ oh. __

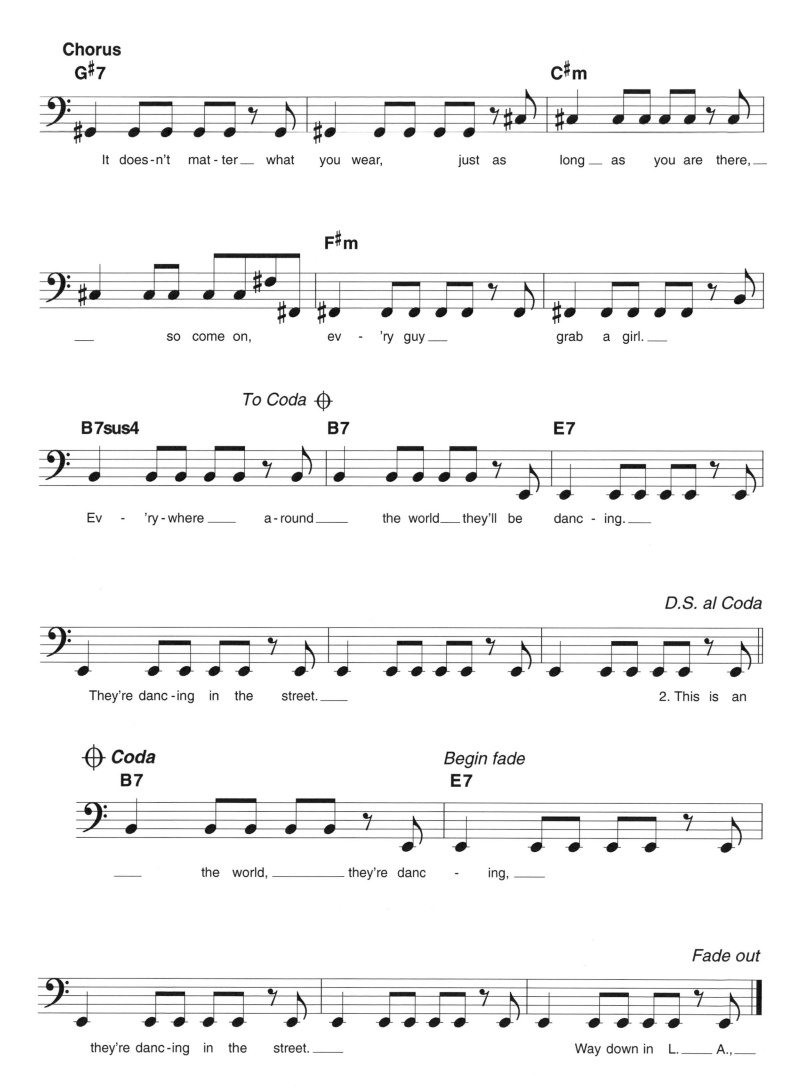

FRIENDS IN LOW PLACES

Words and Music by
DeWAYNE BLACKWELL and EARL BUD LEE

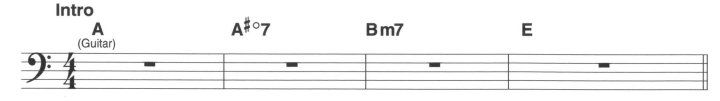

1. Blame it

fear in his eyes ___ when I took his glass ___ of cham-pagne. ___ Then
___ a big scene. ___ Just give me an ho-ur and then, well,

I toast-ed you, __ said, "Hon-ey, we may be through, __ but you'll nev-er hear ___ me com-plain."
I'll be as high __ as that i - vo - ry tow - er _____ that you're liv-in' in. __

Chorus

'Cause I got friends ___ in ___ low plac - es where the

whis-key drowns ___ and the beer chas - es my blues ____ a-way, ___

and I'll be o - kay. ___ Yeah,

I'm not big ___ on so - cial grac - es. Think I'll slip on down ___ to the

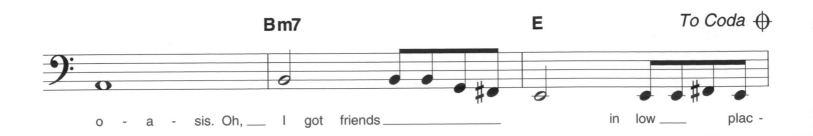

Bm7   E   *To Coda* ⊕

o - a - sis. Oh, __ I got friends _____ in low ____ plac -

Guitar Solo

A   A

es.

D.S. al Coda

Bm7   E   A

2. Well, I

⊕ *Coda*   **Outro-Chorus**

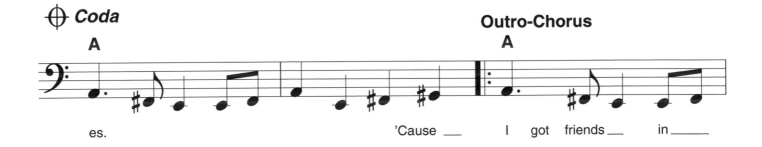

A   A

es.   'Cause __ I got friends __ in _____

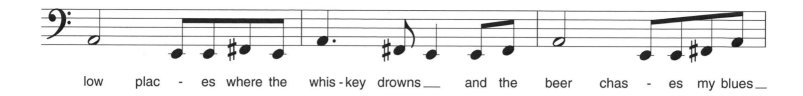

low plac - es where the whis - key drowns ___ and the beer chas - es my blues __

Bm7　　　　　　　　　　　　　　　**E**

___ a - way, ___　　　　　　　　and I'll　be o - kay. ___

A

Yeah,　I'm not big ___ on　so - cial grac - es. Think I'll

Bm7

slip on down ___ to the o - a - sis. Oh, ___ I got friends _____

E　　　　　　　　　　　**A**　　　　　　　　　*Repeat and fade*

in low ___ plac - es.　　　　　　　　　　　'Cause ___

CROSSFIRE

Written by BILL CARTER,
RUTH ELLSWORTH, REESE WYNANS,
TOMMY SHANNON and CHRIS LAYTON

Melody:

Day by day,   night af - ter night,

Intro
N.C.(E7)

Verse
Play 3 times   **N.C.(E7)**

1. Day by day,   night af - ter night,

blind - ed by   the ne - on lights,   hur - ry here,

hus - tl - in' there,   no one's got   the time to spare.

Mon - ey's tight,   noth - in' free.

Won't some-bod - y come and res - cue _____ me? I am strand -

Chorus
N.C. (E7♯9)

- ed, _____ caught in _____ the cross - fire.

Strand -ed, _____ caught in the cross-fire._

Verse
N.C.(E7)

_____ 2. Tooth for tooth,

eye for an eye, _____ sell your soul _____ just to buy, buy, _____ buy. _____

Beg -gin' a dol - lar, steal - in' a dime, _____ come on can't ya see

BORN UNDER A BAD SIGN

Words and Music by
BOOKER T. JONES and WILLIAM BELL

Melody:

Born _____ un - der a bad _____ sign.

Intro
C#7

% Chorus
C#7

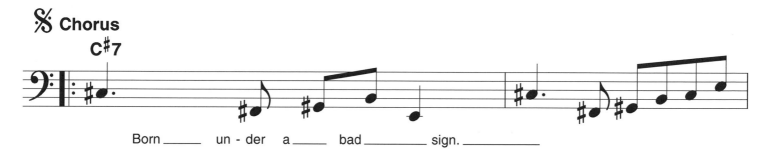

Born _____ un - der a _____ bad _____ sign. _____

To Coda ⊕

Been down _____ since I be - gan to crawl.

G#7   **F#7**

If it was - n't for bad _____ luck,   you know I would - n't have no   luck at

C#7   **Verse**
                          C#7

all.   1. Hard luck and trou - ble
                                        2. I can't read, _____

SMOKE ON THE WATER

Words and Music by RITCHIE BLACKMORE,
IAN GILLAN, ROGER GLOVER,
JON LORD and IAN PAICE

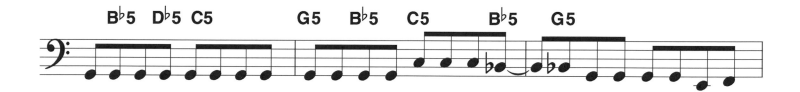

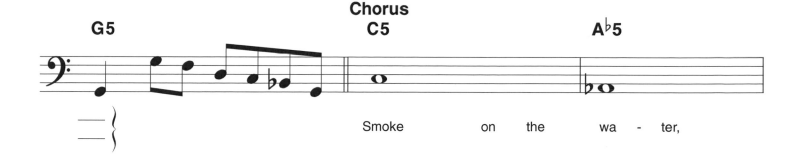

Chorus

Smoke on the wa - ter,

a fire ___ in the sky. ___ Smoke on the

Interlude

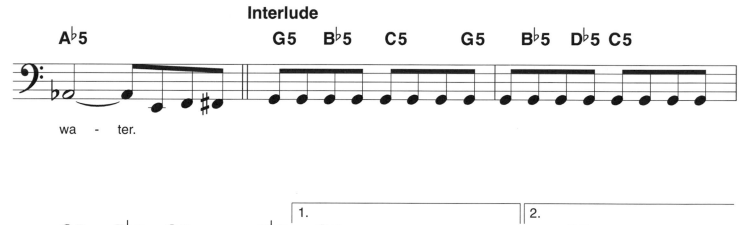

wa - ter.

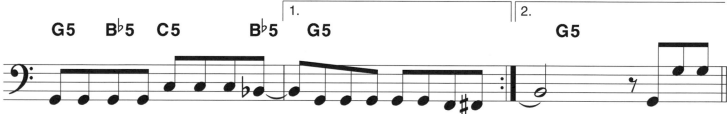

Outro-Organ Solo

Repeat and fade

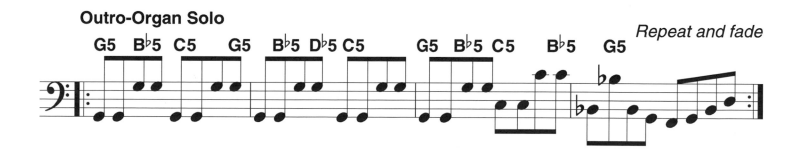

HAL LEONARD BASS METHOD

HAL LEONARD BASS METHOD BOOK 1
SECOND EDITION
BY ED FRIEDLAND

METHOD BOOKS

by Ed Friedland

BOOK 1
Book 1 teaches: tuning; playing position; musical symbols; notes within the first five frets; common bass lines, patterns and rhythms; rhythms through eighth notes; playing tips and techniques; more than 100 great songs, riffs and examples; and more! The audio includes 44 full-band tracks for demonstration or play-along.
00695067 Book Only.......................................$7.99
00695068 Book/Online Audio...............................$12.99

BOOK 2
Book 2 continues where Book 1 left off and teaches: the box shape; moveable boxes; notes in fifth position; major and minor scales; the classic blues line; the shuffle rhythm; tablature; and more!
00695069 Book Only.......................................$7.99
00695070 Book/Online Audio...............................$12.99

BOOK 3
With the third book, progressing students will learn more great songs, riffs and examples; sixteenth notes; playing off chord symbols; slap and pop techniques; hammer-ons and pull-offs; playing different styles and grooves; and more.
00695071 Book Only.......................................$7.99
00695072 Book/Online Audio...............................$12.99

COMPOSITE
This money-saving edition contains Books 1, 2 and 3.
00695073 Book Only.......................................$17.99
00695074 Book/Online Audio...............................$24.99

DVD
Play your favorite songs in no time with this DVD! Covers: tuning, notes in first through third position, rhythms through eighth notes, fingerstyle and pick playing, 4/4 and 3/4 time, and more! Includes 6 full songs and on-screen music notation. 68 minutes.
00695849 DVD...$19.95

BASS FOR KIDS
by Chad Johnson
Bass for Kids is a fun, easy course that teaches children to play bass guitar faster than ever before. Popular songs such as "Crazy Train," "Every Breath You Take," "A Hard Day's Night" and "Wild Thing" keep kids motivated, and the clean, simple page layouts ensure their attention remains focused on one concept at a time.
00696449 Book/Online Audio $12.99

REFERENCE BOOKS

BASS SCALE FINDER
by Chad Johnson
Learn to use the entire fretboard with the *Bass Scale Finder*. This book contains over 1,300 scale diagrams for the most important 17 scale types.
00695781 6" x 9" Edition.................................$7.99
00695778 9" x 12" Edition................................$7.99

BASS ARPEGGIO FINDER
by Chad Johnson
This extensive reference guide lays out over 1,300 arpeggio shapes. 28 different qualities are covered for each key, and each quality is presented in four different shapes.
00695817 6" x 9" Edition.................................$7.99
00695816 9" x 12" Edition................................$7.99

MUSIC THEORY FOR BASSISTS
by Sean Malone
Acclaimed bassist and composer Sean Malone will explain the written language of music, using easy-to-understand terms and concepts, diagrams, and much more. The audio provides 96 tracks of examples, demonstrations, and play-alongs.
00695756 Book/Online Audio $17.99

STYLE BOOKS

BASS LICKS
by Ed Friedland
This comprehensive supplement to any bass method will help students learn over 200 great bass licks, lines and grooves in many rhythmic styles. *Bass Licks* illustrates how simple melodic patterns can become the springboard for group improvisation or the foundation of a song.
00696035 Book/Online Audio $14.99

BASS LINES
by Matt Scharfglass
500 expertly written bass lines, riffs and fills in a wide variety of musical genres are included in this comprehensive collection to help players expand their bass vocabulary. The examples cover many tempos, keys and feels, and include easy bass lines for beginners on up to advanced riffs for more experienced bassists.
00148194 Book/Online Audio $19.99

BLUES BASS
by Ed Friedland
Learn to play studying the songs of B.B. King, Stevie Ray Vaughan, Muddy Waters, Albert King, the Allman Brothers, T-Bone Walker, and many more. Learn riffs from blues classics including: Born Under a Bad Sign • Hideaway • Hoochie Coochie Man • Killing Floor • Pride and Joy • Sweet Home Chicago • The Thrill Is Gone • and more.
00695870 Book/Online Audio $14.99

COUNTRY BASS
by Glenn Letsch
21 songs, including: Act Naturally • Boot Scootin' Boogie • Crazy • Honky Tonk Man • Love You Out Loud • Luckenbach, Texas (Back to the Basics of Love) • No One Else on Earth • Ring of Fire • Southern Nights • Streets of Bakersfield • Whose Bed Have Your Boots Been Under? • and more.
00695928 Book/Online Audio $17.99

FRETLESS BASS
by Chris Kringel
18 songs, including: Bad Love • Continuum • Even Flow • Everytime You Go Away • Hocus Pocus • I Could Die for You • Jelly Roll • King of Pain • Kiss of Life • Lady in Red • Tears in Heaven • Very Early • What I Am • White Room • more.
00695850...$19.99

FUNK BASS
by Chris Kringel
This is your complete guide to learning the basics of grooving and soloing funk bass. Songs include: Can't Stop • I'll Take You There • Let's Groove • Stay • What Is Hip • and more.
00695792 Book/Online Audio..............................$22.99

R&B BASS
by Glenn Letsch
This book/audio pack uses actual classic R&B, Motown, soul and funk songs to teach you how to groove in the style of James Jamerson, Bootsy Collins, Bob Babbitt, and many others. The 19 songs include: For Once in My Life • Knock on Wood • Mustang Sally • Respect • Soul Man • Stand by Me • and more.
00695823 Book/Online Audio $17.99

ROCK BASS
by Sean Malone
This book/audio pack uses songs from a myriad of rock genres to teach the key elements of rock bass. Includes: Another One Bites the Dust • Beast of Burden • Money • Roxanne • Smells like Teen Spirit • and more.
00695801 Book/Online Audio..............................$21.99

SUPPLEMENTARY SONGBOOKS

These great songbooks correlate with Books 1-3 of the *Hal Leonard Bass Method*, giving students great songs to play while they're still learning! The audio tracks include great accompaniment and demo tracks.

EASY POP BASS LINES
20 great songs that students in Book 1 can master. Includes: Come as You Are • Crossfire • Great Balls of Fire • Imagine • Surfin' U.S.A. • Takin' Care of Business • Wild Thing • and more.
00695810 Book Only......................................$9.99
00695809 Book/Online Audio..............................$15.99

MORE EASY POP BASS LINES
20 great songs for Level 2 students. Includes: Bad, Bad Leroy Brown • Crazy Train • I Heard It Through the Grapevine • My Generation • Pride and Joy • Ramblin' Man • Summer of '69 • and more.
00695819 Book Only......................................$12.99
00695818 Book/Online Audio..............................$16.99

EVEN MORE EASY POP BASS LINES
20 great songs for Level 3 students, including: ABC • Another One Bites the Dust • Brick House • Come Together • Higher Ground • Iron Man • The Joker • Sweet Emotion • Under Pressure • more.
00695821 Book...$9.99
00695820 Book/Online Audio..............................$16.99

HAL•LEONARD

Visit Hal Leonard online at
www.halleonard.com

Prices, contents and availability subject to change without notice.
Some products may not be available outside of U.S.A.